MW00423394

Praise for *Noble Listening* ...

"A true treasure! When we shift our attention toward listening, our whole world changes. Learning to listen is equal to learning to love. This creative handbook teaches us that learning to listen does not have to be a mystery. Rather, there are tangible ways that we can deepen our capacity for empathy and presence - transforming our relationships with others and ourselves. It has helped me to be a better educator, spouse, and parent. *Noble Listening* is a rare gift indeed!"

~ Ruth Cox, PhD
Institute for Holistic Healing Studies
San Francisco State University

"*Noble Listening* is a delight. It is simple, direct and profound; easy to read and follow. People crave attention and understanding, and this book will help those in all relationships improve their ability to connect, listen and love."

~ Frederic Luskin, PhD
Forgive for Good
Director, Stanford Forgiveness Project

"This delightful little book contains huge treasures, the ones that can bring us back into the joy of being human together. I imagine that if a reader only focused on two or three of the many skills given here, that they would quickly become skilled in listening, and would fall in love with the places that real conversation always takes us."

~ Margaret J. Wheatley
Leadership and the New Science

"Listening is no small skill, and so this little book is no small matter. Everyone who wants better relationships and more productivity should read this. It's fun, easy to read and speaks to the heart of the matter. I think it's a winner."   ~ Richard Carlson, PhD

Don't Sweat the Small Stuff

"The foundation of good teaching is the ability to listen. Although Mark Brady writes for a much broader audience, he has provided an indispensable tool – actually, a great gift – for classroom instructors. I will carry *Noble Listening* in my pocket on a daily basis."

~ Mary Fainsod Katzenstein, PhD
Cornell University

"This book may be little, but the significance of its message is big…very big. With appealing modesty and great sensitivity, Mark Brady offers the reader a wealth of practical tips for how to listen more attentively and effectively to others. If only a fraction of this wise advice could be put into practice, the benefits – for listener and speaker alike – would be enormous."

~ Doug McAdam, PhD
former director, Stanford Center for
Advanced Study in the Behavioral Sciences
Dynamics of Contention

"Reading *Noble Listening* should be required for all human beings, as soon as they can read and as long as their eyesight allows. The fundamentals of listening, articulated so clearly, spell out how to achieve this distinctly human skill. Don't pass up the opportunity to deepen your skill, regardless of your current level of proficiency. We can all become deeper, stronger and better listeners."

~ Joan C. King, PhD
Cellular Wisdom

"When you do what I do for a living, it's rare to find a book that's practical, satisfying, learnable and inspirational all in the same breath. *Noble Listening* is all that and much, much more. Two copies should be issued simultaneously with every marriage license."

~ Peter Pearson, PhD
In Quest of the Mythical Mate
The Couples Institute

Noble Listening

Contemplative practices
for fostering
kindness and compassion

by

Mark Brady, Ph.D.

Paideia* Press
Whidbey Island, WA

Paideia Press
5489 Coles Road
Langley, WA 98260
(360) 981-1410
paideia@gmail.com

***PAIDEIA** (pie-day-a) from the Greek pais, paidos:
lifelong learning that pays special attention
to the spirit, heart or essence of things.

Library of Congress Cataloging-in-Publication Data

Brady, Mark, PhD
Noble Listening / Mark Brady p. cm.

ISBN -10 1-5030197- 4-8
ISBN -13 978-1-5030197-4-8

153.7'7–dc27

2019111946

24 23 22 21 20 19
11 10   9   8   7   6

Designed by Rosework Studios/Muriel Hastings
Cover Photo: © Marilyna | Dreamstime.com - Zen Beauty
"When Someone Listens Deeply to You" used with
permission - John Fox - Institute for Poetic Medicine
Printed in the United States of America

WHEN SOMEONE DEEPLY LISTENS TO YOU

When someone deeply listens to you
it is like holding out a dented cup
you've had since childhood
and watching it fill up with
cold, fresh water.
When it balances on top of the brim,
you are understood.
When it overflows and touches your skin,
you are loved.

When someone deeply listens to you
the room where you stay
starts a new life
and the place where you wrote
your first poem
begins to glow in your mind's eye.
It is as if gold has been discovered!

When someone deeply listens to you
your bare feet are on the earth
and a beloved land that seemed distant
is now at home within you.

~ John Fox

How to get the most out of this book

The practices in this little book truly are life-changing and love-affirming. As such, they often need to be read and worked with regularly, essentially using listening as a contemplative practice. I suggest you read the titles and mark those that first resonate with you. Begin with those skills and practice them in any way that feels comfortable.

You may wish to carry this book with you and refer to it often as you begin practicing new skills. Feel free to write in the book and take notes. Be creative in doing whatever you need to get the most out of these practices.

One way to get the most out of *Noble Listening* is to create a community of practice. Ask friends, family, colleagues, or members of your sangha or faith community to practice with you. Small, contemplation groups have been quite effective in helping each other learn to listen skillfully. As your listening skills grow, you actually begin putting kindness and compassion into practice.

If you feel anxiety, sorrow, anger or any other strong negative emotion while reading a particular skill, attend carefully to yourself. What is the discomfort about? Perhaps an early life event (see pages 141-145) is being reactivated. It is often useful to turn towards such feelings and learn what they may have to teach you, but do not force a practice that is overly charged for you. Take your time. Be curious. Play. Have fun while you learn a powerful practice - the art of noble listening.

Table of Contents

Introduction

"I just need you to listen to me."   *Page 23*

27. Learn to let go ✓   me + ivan
28. Listen between the words
29. Champion the timid voice
30. Listen for inconsistencies
31. Listen with a soft belly
32. Return to the needs of the present moment
33. Develop methods for skillful self-listening
34. Cultivate patience
35. Become someone who can hear hard truths
36. Be mindful of age, race and gender bias ✓
37. Break the "I" habit
38. Ask specific, clarifying questions
39. Say what's useful; say what's true

Introduction

Hearing is one of the first senses born to us and the last to die. Recent neuroscience research confirms that this is no random event. It is the energy of sound, in particular, the sound of mother's voice, that largely fuels our *in utero* development.[1] The healing power of being listened to has been recognized for centuries, and there's good evidence to suggest that listening continues to help increase the numbers and connections of neurons in the brain, very likely throughout the lifespan.[2]

Many of us know the exquisite feeling of being listened to by a skillful listener – that is, feeling deeply heard, appreciated, accepted and understood. Being listened to enlivens us and inspires opportunities to explore what we think, how we feel, what we want, who we are, and who we're becoming. It is an experience with many benefits.

But if being listened to holds such tremendous benefits, why learn to be a good listener as opposed to being a good speaker? In this little book you'll discover the many benefits – both subtle and obvious – that are equally available to a skilled listener.

Listening mindfully grows our brains and feeds our hearts. It invites us to "put others at the center," and allows us to create better relationships with colleagues and loved ones. Predictably, skilled listeners experience more joy, peace and ease in their lives. They acquire tools to practice forgiveness and express gratitude. New perspectives on life's challenges reveal themselves as skillful listeners learn rich and precious things about other human beings, and in the process, about themselves being human.

The world needs more skilled listeners, but moreover, it needs the opened hearts of those who become truly skilled in this practice. It needs the ways in which skilled listeners look to make peace. It needs the mindful questions that skilled listeners ask themselves, as well as the questions we ask others, such as, "What hurts?" "What are you struggling with?" and "How can I help?"

Over many years, I have come to experience and think of listening as a contemplative practice, one that many readers of my previous five books feel has been instrumental in helping them to connect deeply with family, friends, business colleagues and themselves as they worked to heal painful personal histories and began moving their lives in positive new directions.

Noble Listening practitioners invite others to speak truthfully and hold the things they hear sacred. Such listeners do not necessarily try to change things, fix them, or run away from them. They learn to pay close attention, and consider Noble Listening an important component of Right Speech, Buddha's first prescription for ethical conduct. They work to become people to whom the tenderest truths may be fearlessly told.

Here in this little book then, are some tools that will help you learn to hear such truths, learn to listen deeply to yourself and to other people. May you be blessed and surrounded by people who love and trust you enough to tell you who they really are all along this timeless journey.

Mark Brady
Whidbey Island, WA
January, 2019

"Being listened to is so close to being loved that most people don't know the difference."

~ David Augsburger

There is a voice that doesn't use words. Listen.

"I just need you to listen to me."

A young black South African woman taught some of my friends a profound lesson about listening. She was sitting in a circle of women from many nations and each woman had the chance to tell a story from her life.

When her turn came, she began quietly to tell a story of true horror – of how she had found her grandparents slaughtered in their village. Many of the women were Westerners, and in the presence of such pain, they instinctively wanted to do something. They wanted to fix it, to make it better, anything to remove the pain of this tragedy from such a young life.

The young woman felt their compassion, but also felt them closing in. She put her hands up, as if to push back their desire to help. She said, "I don't need you to fix me. I just need you to listen to me."

She taught many women that day that being listened to is enough. If we can speak our story and know that others truly hear it, we are somehow healed by that. During the Truth and Reconciliation Commission hearings in South Africa, many who testified to the atrocities they had endured under apartheid would speak of being healed by their own testimony. They knew that many people were listening to their story.

One young man who had been blinded when a policeman shot him in the face at close range said, "I feel what has brought my eyesight back is to come here and tell the story. I feel what has been making me sick all this time is the fact that I couldn't tell my story. But now it feels like I've got my sight back by coming here and telling you the story."

~ Margaret Wheatley

1. Talk less

This is the simplest and fastest change we can make on the road to becoming a Noble Listener. In conversations with others, we can pay attention to who's doing most of the talking. If it's not us, that's a good start. From here, we can employ a host of additional skills that can improve our listening even further.

However, if *we* are doing most of the talking, there are practices we can do to shift the balance toward listening more. The first thing is to notice ourselves talking and not listening. Without this primary awareness, little else can happen. *With* this awareness, a number of options become possible. First of all, we now have the choice to decide to stop talking. There are many ways to accomplish this. We might ask questions such as, "What's your sense?" "What's on your mind?" "I'm interested in your thoughts. Please say more."

There are additional means and methods for passing conversations over to others as well. Smiling or nodding encourages others to talk. A simple statement like, "I have been doing most of the talking; I'll stop now and listen," is a direct invitation for others to speak. The possibilities for gracefully shifting from speaking to listening are limitless. Make up any that you feel comfortable with and practice using them.

Becoming a Noble Listener starts first with the intention to talk less and listen more. Learning to stop talking so much and to listen is a powerful step in loving ourselves and other people. In a world full of talkers, a skillful listener shines like a bodhisattva reciting the Diamond Sutra.

Practice: *Identify someone with whom you often do most of the talking. Utilize at least one skill from this book to swing the balance toward them talking more. What's the experience like?* Noah

2. Don't interrupt unnecessarily Pick this we to serbian culture

Many times, as we're listening to another person, the things they say will emotionally activate us in some way. Their words may trigger excitement, sadness, fear or some other strong feeling. Such feelings can gen-

erate the uncontrollable impulse to speak, to
override what the other person is saying in
order to relieve our own internal tension. This
is another one of those impulses – like letting
your story take over another's (Skill No. 18) –
that's important to harness on the road to
becoming a more skillful listener. When we
cut people off in mid-sentence or interrupt by
finishing their thoughts out loud, we're being
disrespectful, and we could be harming our
own health! Dr. Paul Pearsall, the author of
The Last Self-Help Book You'll Ever Need
writes, "Stop expressing, representing, and
asserting yourself. Shut up and listen." *– Naam says it*

 Research shows that people who interrupt
are three times more likely to die of a heart
attack than those who don't, and that (relationships) usually fail because of too much
communication, not too little."[4]

When we interrupt, the message we send
to the speaker is "What I have to say is more
important than what you have to say. It's so
important that I simply can't contain myself
enough to let you finish." By learning to hold
our tongue in daily interactions with people,
and becoming genuinely curious about what

others are saying, we greatly improve our listening skills and possibly our own health.

Practice: Pay attention to how frequently you and other people interrupt one another in everyday communication. Take steps to reduce your own pattern of interrupting and notice the positive effect it has on the way they relate to you. For example, one step you can take is to place your tongue against the roof of your mouth and hold it there.

3. Promote an atmosphere of trust

Communication that meaningfully connects people occurs when trust exists. A good listener works skillfully to build and maintain trust. This means not putting others on guard – erecting psychological defenses –and having a genuine concern for their comfort and well-being.

There are many ways to establish trust. Most effective is to be genuinely trustworthy. Trustworthy people rarely betray trust. When your central concern is for the safety and well-being of yourself and others, often there is nothing special that needs to be done. Many people intuitively sense this authentic orientation.

Although we like to think we are trustworthy, sometimes old patterns of behavior, shaped by early life events (see pages 141-145), can cause us to allow unconscious needs, wants and desires to prevent us from fully concerning ourselves with the care and safety of others. Such early life events can keep us from taking good care of ourselves as well. Learning about the things that may be getting in the way of skillful listening, as well as being able to promote an environment of trust, is vitally important to each of us. If genuine trust is to be established, such influence from early life events needs to be compassionately brought into the light of day, skillfully worked with, and fully resolved.

Practice: Who are the people you feel safe enough to tell your deepest truths to? Which are the elements that contribute most significantly to that feeling? What's one thing you might do to move more in the direction of being someone others deeply trust?

4. Listen disrespect – fully

Think of your last conflict or disagreement. You may not be able to clearly recall exactly what it was about, but it's very likely you can recall how you felt. That's because the seeming cause of many conflicts – the unkept promise, the misunderstood perspective or the missed appointment – is not really what's at the heart of the matter.

Whenever conflict arises, one of two things is often taking place. (I'll discuss the second one in the next practice.) In daily life many people know they feel unhappy, or angry, but they fail to realize deep down they're feeling disrespected. Disrespect is a tricky emotion. We can feel disrespected even though a speaker might not feel they are being disrespectful. What are we to do if disrespect can be easily triggered, but not easily identified?

A skillful listener looks and listens for signs of another person feeling disrespected. Some common signs are expressions of anger or sarcasm, verbal attacks, hostile body language, or refusing to communicate. A skillful listener inquires about these observations and asks if disrespect is an issue. Permitting the speaker time to think beyond their surface feelings, helps allow room for feelings of disrespect to be identified. Once disrespect has been identified, the listener can move forward to work towards a solution or make authentic amends that may be necessary.

Practice: *Listen for the clues in the next conflict you find yourself in that indicate whether you and others may be feeling disrespected. Once that issue is identified, a whole host of creative possibilities becomes available for authentically addressing the real cause. Once the real issue – evoked feelings of disrespect – is resolved, coming to agreement and resolving conflicts involving secondary concerns becomes much more workable.*

5. Listen for mutual purpose

The second cause of many conflicts is a lack or loss of mutual purpose. Until mutual purposes are identified or reaffirmed, very few conflicts will ever be readily resolved.

Even the most bitter of enemies, by simple virtue of their common humanity, have mutual purposes in common, i.e. survival needs, self-esteem needs and the need for respect. What "enemies" are often in conflict over, especially in business and personal relationships, are the best ways to get such needs met. However, if respect can be developed between people working at odds, then a foundation will exist for exploring and/or re-establishing mutual purpose.

Differences may still exist, but the possibility for coming to agreement is significantly enhanced if mutual respect and common purpose are identified and set solidly in place.

Listening for mutual purpose then, is done by first hearing all the ways people are working at cross-purposes. A skillful listener then listens for the places where mutual purpose might be hiding in the conflict. This does not mean that resolving conflict is easy and won't require hard work, but by focusing on mutual respect and mutual purpose, a skillful listener will be addressing the things that can constructively make conflict resolution a possibility.

Practice: *The next time you find yourself in a conflict with someone, look for any cross-purposes that may exist. Then look for where a discussion of mutual purpose might begin. It may even be fruitful to ask the other person where they see both of you operating on the same page. You can begin from there.*

6. Be slow to disagree, argue or criticize

Under stress, many conversations become laced with criticism, argument and disagreement. When we engage in these behaviors as a listener, we can't hear what the other person is trying to say. Attempting to force our point across keeps us from hearing any underlying needs wanting to be expressed. A skillful listener listens to others beliefs, points of view and versions of truth. It may be hard to hear things we don't like (Skill No. 35), things we might want to change, but skillful listening allows the speaker full rein to say whatever they may need to say.

Using other listening skills recommended in this book can help put an end to argument, criticism and disagreement. It takes discernment and practice to be open to things that are difficult to hear or what we think needs to be corrected, but in the long run, any bottom-line truth that has room to emerge from another person is worth far more than "being right," or "changing another's mind." Being slow to disagree, argue or criticize goes a long way to allow truth, understanding and compassion to organically unfold.

Practice: Observe several different conver-sations over the next few days. Listen for how much argument, disagreement, or criticism passes for conversation. Pay particular attention to its effect on your body – how it makes you feel. How does it affect your breathing? Heart rate? Sensations in the pit of your stomach?

7. Pay attention to the need for control

How many times have you observed or taken part in a conversation where two or more people are talking at the same time? If such a situation goes on for any duration, each participant will keep raising his or her voice, trying to out-decibel the other until it actually becomes quite comical.

In such situations very little listening is occurring, and a power struggle is taking place, even though that might not be so obvious to the participants. In fact, many exchanges that pass as dialogues are really exercises in one-upmanship and competition for control of the conversation. The irony is, in many conversations it is the *listener* who potentially holds the greatest power by virtue of what he or she chooses to ignore or respond to. By electing to selectively attend to content and focus on emotional tone or immediate context, a skillful listener can turn a conversation or conflict 180 degrees in a matter of moments.

Many people are reluctant to give over control in a discussion for fear that it is something given over forever or that it signifies weakness. The biblical injunction to "seek first to understand, and then to be understood" is good advice. It's not only possible, but advantageous to temporarily give the floor over to another. Once a person has had the opportunity to express what they need to, frequently they have more energy available to pay attention to what you have to say. As it is written in an ancient book of wisdom: "Yield and overcome."

Practice: Observe people in conversation over the course of several days. Who does most of the talking? Who interrupts? Can you see where the balance of control lies? Are you aware of any control issues in your own conversations? With whom and over what? What do you need most to manage in yourself in these interactions?

8. Cultivate "Beginner's Ear"

Beginner's Ear is a way of paying attention to the present moment that is open and curious. It holds a sense of wonder and delight and the possibility of discovery in the midst of focusing on increasingly finer detail.

To gain a sense of what Beginner's Ear might be like, we can think of how the sounds of the world affected us as a small child. We can recall what it was like on a warm summer night and we heard that very first cricket chirp and then heard smaller details – the rhythm, the silence between chirps, and the answering call of the other crickets.

Other sounds of childhood might also help us recall the feel and flavor of Beginner's Ear. Everything was new and thrilling because we were curious, slowed things down, and paid close attention to what had captured our fancy. It is paying close attention to ever-finer detail that comprises the core of Beginner's Ear. Attention to discriminating detail is the remedy that literally works best to keep things from "going in one ear and out the other."

Practice: Hold a conversation with someone you regularly talk to. Listen with a new sense of curiosity and wonder. What are some things you hear that you may not have heard before? What does curiosity feel like in your body? What does wonder and delight feel like in your chest? In your head? In your heart?

9. Get comfortable with silence

The plain and simple truth is that few of us are perfectly comfortable with silence. We live and work with radios and TVs blaring. We use cell phones and carry on conversations in spaces that used to be silent and sacred. The extinction of silence is taking place all over the world, right before our very ears.

Becoming comfortable with silence is a necessary and critical aspect of skillful listening. It is in the silent spaces inside ourselves, or between two people in dialogue, that deeper, more creative ideas begin to emerge. In silence, something bordering on magic transpires: as a listener we offer others a chance to discover what they think, how they feel, what they want. The same is true when we listen in silence to ourselves. In silence, we can listen and discover what's required to live more fully. MIT organizational scientist and co-author of *Presence*, Peter Senge identifies this as "generative listening" – the art of developing deeper silences that work to slow the ear's hearing to the mind's natural speed.

One way to become increasingly comfortable with silence is to spend increasing amounts of time with it. As we do, silence's rhythms and sensations will become intimately familiar to us. It is, after all, this spacious emptiness at the sub-atomic level that quantum physicists tell us mostly makes up who we are!

Practice: *Make it a point to be aware of how silence in a conversation feels to you. Does it cause anxiety? Do you automatically rush to fill the space? Be mindful of the quiet and see if you can allow silence to be a part of your conversations, a time to sit and reflect on what the speaker has told you, a time to honor and hold what has been said.*

10. Manage emotional reactivity

Nothing stops another person from saying what they really want to say faster than unbridled emotional reactivity such as speaking in loud, angry tones, replying with sarcasm, personal attacks, or even fuming in stifled silence. Emotional reactivity not only interferes with listening, it can seriously damage a relationship. It undermines trust and is disrespectful. Unchecked emotional reactivity inhibits clear, creative thinking and limits uncovering the hidden potential present in almost all situations and every interaction.

Those who frequently communicate in this reactive fashion say, "That's just the way I am. Don't take it personally." Such justification demonstrates little real understanding of reactivity's powerful negative impact on the communication process. However, lack of awareness doesn't mean that the negative impact is not happening just the same.

At the root of all reactivity may be a behavior pattern based upon old wounds from times when we've felt belittled, humiliated, misunderstood or disrespected ourselves (See pages 141-145). Making peace with and healing these old wounds is important work for a skillful listener. Some people will argue, "I don't have control over what I say. Things just pop out of my mouth." The work of a skillful listener is to learn how to skillfully act in *response* to the thoughts that fuel the emotional reactivity behind the words, and work toward healing internal wounds.

Practice: *Spend some time during the coming week noticing the power that others' words have to move you reactively. Notice things that trigger you. What needs of yours might be going unfulfilled? What fears or concerns might such a speaker be triggering? Can you find a positive way to get such fears alleviated or your own needs met?*

11. Avoid "shoulding" on people

Sometimes we find ourselves offering other people unsolicited advice. As well-meaning as we may be, unless it's specifically asked for, advice doesn't work. It's rarely heeded and seldom needed. Living inside each of us is a wealth of embodied wisdom and experience that is much more reliable, insightful and trustworthy than any advice that might be offered by someone else. Telling people what they "should" do, at best, runs interference, blocking access to this internal wisdom. At worst, "shoulding" on people ends up being judgmental and disrespectful and often makes them feel unsafe. It also often leaves us saddled with the responsibility to fix others problems. And while our solutions might work perfectly for us, they won't necessarily work that way for someone else.

A more skillful listening response when we find ourselves tempted to tell people what they "should" do, is to reflect back and ask Strategic Questions in an attempt to put people in touch with their own inner wise counsel (Skill No. 44). "What does your gut tell you?" "If you're of two minds, what is each telling you?" "What outcome would be optimal in this situation?" Continually inviting others to look to themselves, to take initiative and set intentions, will go a long way toward making everyone's life easier.

Practice: For the next week, pay attention to the ways you are tempted to give advice to others. Notice what your motivation might be for doing so. What might you offer in lieu of advice? Practice skillful ways of returning the responsibility, ability and creative energy for solving problems back to them.

12. Stop when your energy flags

Like many human endeavors, listening skillfully takes work and expends energy. The amount of energy we can direct to it at any one time can vary considerably. Available energy is variable and influenced by a whole host of factors, both known and unknown. But one thing is clear: our available energy waxes and wanes through the course of a day.

Interacting with people often saps our vitality, particularly with "energy vampires" – those people who have the mysterious capacity to drain off our energy and soak it up like a sponge. At times, with people like this and others, when our ability to listen fully is flagging, a skillful listener takes responsibility and finds ways to convey respect and concern for another, while at the same time limiting or cutting short a meeting or conversation. Rather than trying to push through when the tank is empty, we can recognize and confess that we don't have sufficient energy to give others our fullest attention. The odds of a satisfying interaction and outcome are much higher when our batteries are fully charged, thus making it critically important to honor our own limitations.

Practice: *Notice in conversations when your energy flags and you begin to tune out the speaker. Experiment with speaking the truth about your inability to listen fully on an "empty tank." Consider the compassionate act of putting off important conversations to a later time when you are more alert and more fully energized.*

13. Establish support for speaking truth to power

It is often difficult to speak truthfully to people who hold power over us. Skillful listeners know this and take it to heart when listening to subordinates. Whether it is a child, employee, or a student, skillful listeners encourage those they hold power over to feel empowered to say what's true with no fear of reprisal. As such they support *satyagraha* – the peaceful force for truth identified by Gandhi.

A satyagraha listener can be present with compassion, willing to hear another's truth and hold it gently, no matter how distressing the truth may be. The Lakota warrior and wise man, Crazy Horse, warned, "Power must listen with honest ears to the whispers of the powerless." To become known for being someone to whom people can speak the truth, you must be kind. You must know that your power makes it difficult for others to speak openly and truthfully unless you deliberately do things to make it happen.

One obvious guideline for those of us holding the responsibility of power is to refrain at all times from ridiculing, blaming, shaming, or condemning. By doing so we establish ourselves as someone who welcomes the truth no matter how disturbing or how poorly expressed it might be. Thus, we build a flawless reputation for welcoming and cherishing truth-tellers. We become trust-worthy people whom others can count on.

Practice: *Notice in the coming weeks, any-time you have the impulse to lie, either by commission or omission. What is the fear that* *underlies it? What might work to permit you to tell the truth? Also, notice how those in subordinate positions speak to you. Can you tell when someone might be telling you what he or she thinks you want to hear, rather than the whole truth and nothing but the truth?*

Section One Reflection Questions

Of these first 13 skills, which stand out the most as I practice to become a skilled listener?

What have I heard that I haven't been able to hear before I began practicing these skills?

I am working to create an atmosphere of trust by...

Notes to myself...

*"We do not believe in ourselves
until someone reveals that something
deep inside us is valuable,
worth listening to,
worthy of our trust,
sacred to our touch."*

~ *e. e. cummings*

"Listen and understand me"

When I ask you to listen and you start giving advice, you have not done what I asked. When I ask you to listen and you start telling me why I shouldn't feel the way I do, you are invalidating my feelings. When I ask you to listen and you start trying to solve my problems, I feel underestimated and disempowered.

When I ask you to listen and you start telling me what I need to do I feel offended, pressured and controlled. When I ask you to listen, it does not mean I am helpless. I may be faltering or discouraged, but I am not helpless. When I ask you to listen and you do things that I can and do need to do for myself, you hurt my self-esteem.

But when you accept the way I feel, then I don't need to spend time and energy trying to defend myself or convince you, and I can focus on figuring out why I feel the way I feel and what to do about it. And when I do that, I don't need advice, just support, trust and encouragement. Please remember that what you think are irrational feelings always makes sense if you take the time to listen and understand me.

~ An adolescent's plea to adults

14. Regularly practice kenosis

Listening is more than simply taking in the words another person says. It often includes a requirement for us to empty our hearts and minds of personal agendas in order to directly connect with another. There's a wonderful Greek word that describes this process perfectly: *kenosis.*

Kenosis comes from *kengo,* which has several related meanings. The primary meaning for skilled listening is "to empty oneself." It is an empty, open state that allows for high levels of listening. It's a state often touched on in meditation.

M. Scott Peck, noted author of *The Road Less Traveled* says, "… the setting aside of one's own prejudices, frames of reference and desires so as to experience as far as possible the speaker's world from the inside, steps inside his or her shoes. This unification of speaker and listener is actually an extension and enlargement of ourselves, and new knowledge is always gained from this. Moreover, since true listening involves a setting aside of the self, it also temporarily involves a total acceptance of the other.

Sensing this acceptance, the speaker will feel less and less vulnerable, and more and more inclined to open up the inner recesses of his or her mind to the listener. As this happens, speaker and listener begin to appreciate each other more and more, and the dance of love is begun again." Peck's description is a wonderful example of kenosis in action.

Practice: Do your best to listen to someone without any agenda – not such an easy thing, since trying to listen without an agenda, is itself an agenda! But do your best to free yourself from your own world and focus on the speaker. Put aside your physical, mental, or emotional aches and pains and focus solely on the other person. Do your best to find out how their world looks and feels. Challenging, isn't it?

15. Listen for feelings

When listening to a speaker's verbal message, the emotion that underlies the message will be most significant. The emotion is what we hear deeply and respond to most strongly, often without even realizing it. Feelings direct us, as speakers and listeners, to deeper truths sitting in the deep structure of language.

Before we can recognize and authentically respond to another's feelings, however, we may be well served to learn to recognize and become comfortable with our own. For some people, this work is like attempting to learn a foreign language, and a difficult one at that.

When we are comfortable knowing what we feel, we will be more easily able to listen better for the emotional content of what another person is saying. When we listen for feelings, we begin to hear things not just with our ears, but with our hearts and bodies as well. It is what the speaker feels that they want us to know and under-stand, even if they can't precisely put it clearly into words.

Practice: How do you know what you feel when you feel it? Spend some time identifying one of the five major feelings: mad, sad, glad, excited, or scared. Notice the place in your body that you predominately experience each feeling. This is a powerful form of self-

listening. Then listen for another person's emotional content. Close your eyes and open your heart to what is really being presented. How would you like best to be received were you in their position?

16. Listen as a caregiver

Listening and understanding is a form of caregiving. Every form of caregiving is treasuring and loving. Whether the caregiving occurs in the form of attending to babies and young children, the lonely, the elderly, the frail and infirm, the disturbed, the dying, or simply caring for the person who next walks in through the front door, each act of caring is an act of love. We know that caring does much to sustain everyday life, even if such acts are not honored or acknowledged. They hold the key to helping us understand how to live together well.

The gift of our complete and focused attention confers on both giver and receiver a sense of meaning and value. When we focus our attention on another, they become more real for us, the relationship becomes more meaningful, and we become naturally more compassionate. The solidity of our sense of "I," obscuring our heart of compassion, begins to dissolve and the "other" becomes our central focus.

If we take a moment to think about it, among the more precious moments in our life are those times when we have felt most deeply understood by another human being.

With attention, we feel heard, seen and understood. We "feel felt." We are nurtured in the gift of another's attention. Giving the gift of our fullest attention gives one of the greatest gifts of all – the gift of noble listening.

Practice: The next time you're in dialogue with someone, focus on the other person with all your senses. What's the "felt sense" you're getting? What's the primary feeling underneath the person's words? What would you be feeling were you in their shoes? How does the gift of your attention seem to affect the other person?

17. Practice the Golden Rule of Listening

The Golden Rule – "Do unto others as you would have them do unto you" – is a time-tested guide for living one's life, one found in all the great spiritual traditions. Listening to others as you would want them to listen to you is excellent guidance as well. There are 51 other skills in this little book, and it's challenging to remember all of them. If you are stumped for a skill to use in a particular situation, use the "Golden Rule of Listening" as your default practice. Keep the intention of the Golden Rule in your heart as you practice other skills as well.

Listen as you would want to be heard. Most people want the listener to hear and understand what they are saying; they want their thoughts and feelings to be known. They want to be able to speak what is true for them and they want that truth to be honored, even if the listener disagrees with their particular expressed version of truth. If we can listen to others by the Golden Rule of Listening, we will be able to hear and connect deeply with others. We will be less inclined to argue, criticize or disagree (Practice No. 6) as we hold the Golden Rule as our guide.

Practice: *This week listen using the Golden Rule of Listening. Do you notice any changes in your listening skills? Do you hear more things or hear them differently than you did before? Can you notice any changes, large or small, in how your circle of friends and acquaintances have been relating to you?*

18. Avoid letting your story take over their story

Often, when we listen to people, what they say strikes a responsive chord in us. We may have had similar thoughts or experiences ourselves. In an attempt to empathize and connect with the person, we may be tempted to tell our own related stories. Resist this impulse.

When we tell our own story, we shift the focus away from the speaker, perhaps for extended periods. Inevitably, this leaves the speaker feeling cut off and frustrated. When this happens, more often than not, the speaker

will stop talking and feel resentful or disrespected, rarely letting you know that directly, of course.

Perhaps the story that you have inter-
rupted is only the beginning of something the
speaker is trying to explore and find their way
more deeply into, or perhaps it is something
they simply need to get off their chest. To
short-circuit this process with your own story
is in a subtle way saying that what you have
to say is more important than what they have
to say. We all know how bad being dismissed
and disrespected feels.

Communication is a creative process
much like writing. Few of us are able to get
everything we want to say down perfectly in
the very first draft. Keeping our story to
ourselves while granting others the floor, is
indeed a listening gift of *dana* – a generosity
of spirit.

*Practice: Next time you find yourself telling
your story in response to someone else's, stop
and apologize for interrupting. Ask the
speaker to please continue. To help get the
speaker back on track, ask a question about*

their story and begin listening anew. Pay attention to how this kind of invitation is acknowledged and received.

19. Check for meaning

Author and researcher, Larry Barker advised skillful listeners to remember, "words have no meaning – people have meaning." Assigning meaning to words is an internal process; meaning comes from inside us. Although our experiences, knowledge and attitudes may differ, we often misinterpret each other's messages, while simultaneously operating under the illusion that a common understanding has been achieved.

It is very difficult not to overlay or add on to what we hear based on our experiences and perceptions. We take the words a person says, filter them through screens of meaning and then draw conclusions or construct interpretations that don't accurately reflect what the speaker intends. Great misunderstandings frequently result.

One way to counter this process is to do regular accuracy checks by repeating or paraphrasing what we think we hear *and* the meaning we make in response to whomever we are listening. Skilled listeners do their best to reflect back a speaker's truth and deeper reality, and not simply a version of their own.

As we experiment with this practice, we can be wrong far more often than right. It takes time to get it right. This is fine so long as we remember that what we're trying to discern is truth and accuracy, and this messy, often cumbersome process is one way to go about it

Practice: In a conversation with someone you trust, explain that you want to practice something "silly" to help you with your listening skills. Ask for permission to reflect back the meaning of what you heard. Ask for feedback. Each time you do this successfully, you hone a great listening skill. You actually learn how to "get" what the other person deeply wants you to know.

20. Listen for content, not delivery

For a variety of reasons, some of us have a hard time saying what we really want to say. We may have a speech impediment or a very slow or very fast way of processing information, or be carrying some form of traumatic history that doesn't permit easy self-expression. Listening to someone who stutters, for example, can be quite challenging. It's difficult not to offer the word the stutterer is stuck on in order to ease our own anxiety.

Other people may talk fast, or slow, or with a heavy accent, or lace their speech with epithets or euphemisms. There are countless ways a speaker can deliver a message that distracts us. Being mindful that the truth lies beyond the content of the message no matter how it is delivered, helps us keep our focus where it needs to be – on the value of the person. We can keep our mind on what is said and who is saying it, not necessarily on how it is said. When we negatively judge someone or his or her message based on their delivery, we lose the content. Moreover, we lose the chance to open our hearts and connect to another. Respectfully listen for content, not delivery, and you will hear far, far more!

Practice: *Identify someone whose style of speech and delivery is difficult for you. Can you remain calm and alert as you pay particular attention to the content of the message? What helps that practice? What hinders it?*

21. Be genuinely curious

Some people are born with a natural inclination to be curious. They ask a lot of questions and explore new things with gusto. These people are more prone to be curious about other people and naturally want to listen and know more about another. Sean Levy, a California Buddhist practitioner, has a way of making everyone he talks to feel extremely important. He gently asks question after question, sincerely wanting to know: "And then what happened?" or "And how did you feel?" His favorite response to a speaker is, "Tell me more."

For those of us not born with a strong inclination to curiousness, we can develop it by remembering what it was like when we were a young child and everything was new and fascinating. When we try on the eyes and ears of a child to encounter our world and the people in it, people whose hearts, brains, minds and bodies are constantly changing, we become more curious about who they are and what they might want us to know.

Curiosity makes us sincerely interested in the person we are listening to. When we are curious, we ask more open-ended questions and are eager for the answers. Our curiosity conveys to a speaker that we care for and appreciate them. Curiosity fuels a desire to lead the speaker deeper and deeper into their truth and invites them to share it with us.

Practice: *Put on "the eyes and ears of a child" the next time you speak with someone. What things do you become curious about? What questions can you ask to discover more about who that person in front of you is right now?*

22. Listen for underlying needs

In one way or another, much human communication is an expression of a need. It may take the direct form of a straightforward request: "Would you present the teaching to the new students this month?" "Do you worry about our finances?" or "May I have a cookie?"

Communication can also indirectly express needs that lie below the surface: "Would you present the teaching?" may mean, "I am too scared/busy/unprepared to do it." "Do you worry about our finances?" may mean, "Something's happening to our money that doesn't make sense?" Or, "May I have a cookie?" may mean "Do you love me?" A skilled listener listens for the underlying needs of the speaker. To get to underlying needs, we can ask a simple question – "Why do you ask?" or "What do you need exactly?" or "Tell me more."

Listening for needs works to identify areas of common interest around which exciting, positive, creative collaborations can be built. For example, if we listen to the colleague who is afraid of presenting the teachings to the new students, we can open up a host of alternative creative possibilities. But it all starts with the realization that virtually all communication is intended to express any variety of needs. The skillful listener is constantly listening for what those needs may be. Ralph Nichols summed it up best when he said, "The most basic of all human needs is the need to understand and be understood. The best way to understand people is to listen to them."[5]

Practice: Things that our friends, family and colleagues need in any communication often are hidden, even from them. Over the next few days, spend some time asking people this simple question: What is it you need?"

23. Identify defensiveness; practice non-defensiveness

When a person we are listening to feels under attack, either rightfully (if an attack can ever be right) or wrongfully, they frequently defend with either silence or violence.

When they react with silence, the conversation stops cold. When they react with violence, either by retaliatory verbal attacks or outright physical assault, this can escalate into even further violence.

Violence can take more subtle forms as well. Sarcastic or snide remarks also have the seeds of violence in them. Any remark that has the effect of diminishing, discounting, belittling, or marginalizing someone has violence at its core.

If we recognize that a defensive response is often rooted in a painful personal history and reactivated by either our behavior or our verbal responses, it can become easier to hear what truths may be lurking under the defensiveness. As such, it's best if we can practice ways of being non-defensive ourselves. If we don't defend against the things that have caused a speaker to react with silence or violence, but rather help the speaker search for what may be causing them to feel attacked. If we believe that skillful listening can truly heal, skillful listeners are open to trying to find the source of pain and make it safe to explore it further.

Defensiveness often begets more conflict. Skillful listeners listen for defensiveness and all the reasons for it, and offer apologies and amends when necessary.

Practice: *Pay attention to the need of others to defend themselves in a conversation. What might you have said or done that triggered the reaction? Do you easily recognize when someone feels the need to defend?*

24. Listen for differences

When we listen to others, often what we listen for are the things we understand or things we agree with. We find comfort in discovering the ways that others are like us. People who are clearly different from us make us uncomfortable. In addition, those whom we thought were very much like us, who turn out to be very different from us, make us uncomfortable as well. We don't like to hear about differences.

A skillful listener deliberately seeks out and pays attention to the ways others are different from us. We begin to appreciate the way human beings have been shaped, molded, and often distorted by culture, schooling, family of origin, genetic makeup, and any number of other unknown factors. Like snowflakes, except at the higher elevations, no two people out of billions and billions are ever exactly alike.

After we've learned to listen for differences and develop an appreciation for them, we can begin to cherish and celebrate our special uniqueness. From this perspective we can turn ourselves into personal and professional planetary citizens, perfectly at home in all our radiant diversity at any place on the planet, and at the same time, we can do the same with others.

Practice: *Spend time paying close attention to things people say that surprise you or that you don't understand or that you disagree with. Consider what you expected them to say. What assumptions underlie your expectations? Can you appreciate how our differences hold the potential to make the world an exciting and interesting place?*

25. Relax and laugh

Learning something new takes time and effort. It's easy to get too caught up in the learning. When that happens, we need to lift our heads up, look around, relax and pay attention to other things in our lives.

There is much to laugh about in learning to skillfully listen. Miscommunication is often the norm. Sometimes, it's a wonder we're able to understand one another at all, especially when we consider that of the 800 English words that people use on a daily basis, each has an average of 17 different meanings! (Other languages the world over, have similar complexities). Add to that the fact that only 35% of a given message's meaning is derived from the actual words we use. These statistics border on the ridiculous, yet it's the reality most of us live with. Learning to be a skillful listener opens the doors to deep understanding and to love, not only for others, but also for ourselves.

However, as with any new skill we take on, we must keep a proper perspective. No matter how hard we try, there will be times when miscommunication happens. We can laugh about it and take whatever necessary steps will lead to greater clarity. The very intention of wanting to be a better listener speaks volumes and is often more important than getting it "perfect."

Practice: *Take some time off from practicing to be a skillful listener and give yourself permission to be "the worst listener in the world!" Relax...enjoy the process of learning*

26. Develop "second attention at the edge"

Growth and learning takes place in people in very much the same way that it does in grass and flowers and trees – right at the edges where the old makes room for the new. In flowers, we observe the tiny openings of buds in springtime displaying the first flash of color. In tree leaves and grasses, we can easily see the darker green as it stands in sharp contrast to the new, brighter green.

Similarly, we can notice such growing hints and contrasts between the old and the emerging new in people. We do that by paying close or "second attention" to those edges where old ways of being and acting are getting ready to fall away, as new areas of expertise and responsibility prepare to burst into bloom.

Often the transitions that growth and change require of us come with some degree of fear and anxiety attached. If we pay respect – look once again, or pay "second attention" – any time we spot hints of fear or anxiety in those around us, we might be curious about the things connected to such fearful concerns. By thinking deeply about creative possibilities in connection with our own and others' growing edges, we can be of enormous help to one another, a practical application of bodhicitta!

Practice: *Look around and listen for changes that might be ready to unfold. In small children, it can be readily apparent as new behaviors appear virtually overnight. What are you hearing that tells you someone may be on the cusp of change and be feeling anxious? How might you best hold sacred the personal truths they might be willing to share with you?*

Section Two Reflection Questions

What changes have I noticed in my relationships since I've begun practicing these listening skills?

What conflicts have I been able to resolve since I've been practicing these skills?

What things am I newly curious about or interested in about other people?

Notes to myself...

"Listening is a magnetic and strange thing, a creative force. . . .When we are listened to, it creates us, makes us unfold and expand. Ideas actually begin to grow within us and come to life."

~ Brenda Ueland
Strength to Your Sword Arm

"What is it you're not saying?"

I had a fascinating experience with a highly balanced masculine and feminine culture two years ago in New Zealand while traveling with a group of women healers. We had been invited to visit a sacred, reservation-like community of the Maori Polynesian culture.

At a gathering of men, women and children, I asked the community's medical doctor just what medicine he used for healing the illnesses on the island. His reply changed my thinking. He said that they used no medicine whatsoever. None.

If a person was sick in any way, from a cold to cancer, they would call the entire community and all gathered round, including the children. They'd position the ill person in the center and the community would sit. This physician would ask the person one question and one question only: "What is it that you are not saying?" They would all sit and wait for days until this person revealed all of what he or she was keeping to him or herself. The doctor reported a ninety-eight percent healing rate. They were using their own innate wisdom, their own inner-guidance and the power of full self-expression, that is, emotional truth, intellectual truth and its interconnectedness.

~ Dr. Christine Hibbard

27. Learn to let go

In many of the previous practices, it's suggested that you open and listen without judging, that you tolerate and accept other people as you find them. Those are tall orders. Each of us has a perspective and a view of the world that makes sense to us. To let go of what we think the world and all the other people in it should be like is challenging. How do we let go?

We may perhaps begin by realizing that the world is made up of billions of people who come from different cultures, who were raised with different parenting styles, and who experienced different early life events that have shaped them into who they are today. In order to let go of our expectations and "shoulds," we must hold fast to the idea of diversity. The world we live in is the result of all of us creating and contributing to things the way they are. When we let go of thinking the world and its inhabitants should be a certain way, we let go of the need for control. We open ourselves and our hearts to what exists without the need to force others to necessarily buy into our worldview.

In a sociological study that interviewed a significant number of people at the end of life, three things were mentioned over and over concerning what made for a rich, complete life: living fully, loving well, and…learning to let go.

Practice: List a dozen ways that you think your life should be different than it is. Next to that list write down how it actually is. Can you love and appreciate and forgive how it actually is, and let go and listen in ways that will allow things to change in directions you'd like them to, without the need for holding on so tightly to how you think it should be?

28. Listen between the words

Skilled listeners pay great attention to what's not being said as well as to what is. They recognize that in many conversations, the speaker is deciding how safe they feel and consequently, what they can painlessly reveal. This process goes on with friends and adversaries alike. Research has demonstrated that the actual words we use convey less than ten percent of the total information that we receive from another. The rest is taken from voice tone, context, body language, and what is *not* said.

Learning to listen for what isn't being said isn't difficult. Body language, stumbling for words, and facial expressions are three things a skilled listener can watch and listen for. As Malcolm Gladwell pointed out in his *New Yorker* article, "The Naked Face," what often isn't being said is readily recognizable to an astute observer simply by looking directly at a speaker's face.[6]

If you suspect something is not being said, ask what will make it safe for someone to say what they might really want to. Then do what is necessary to create that safe place. Author and poet, Charles C. Finn said, "I tell you everything that is really nothing, and nothing of what is everything. Do not be fooled by what I'm saying. Please listen carefully and try to hear what I am not saying."[7]

Remember, being trustworthy, as we noted before, goes a long way in helping others feel safe enough to speak truthfully. By and large, people do want you to hear what it is they are not saying.

Practice: *Over the next few days, observe conversations you have with friends and acquaintances. Ask if there is something that they really want to say, but feel they can't. Ask what you can do to make it safe, so they can tell you what it is they are not saying.*

29. Champion the timid voice

All of us are wiser than any one of us. When two or more people get together, there are gems of wisdom waiting to be discovered. The timid voice doesn't offer up these gems for a variety of reasons. Some may feel it is unsafe to speak. Others might not be clear about what they want to say.

Similar to making it safe for small children to speak freely – great wisdom out of the mouths of babes – when a skilled listener champions the timid voice they take care to convey ongoing respect and provide protection from judgments, criticisms, and ridicule in any form. And not just for the timid voices, but for everyone present all the time. It is often from observing such safe treatment that timid voices will cautiously begin speaking up.

Championing the timid voice is much like creating a safe harbor where people can speak truth to power (Skill No. 13). You may not be in a position of power over the timid voice, but it is still difficult for such shy people to speak up.

When intimidating or overwhelming elements in any situation are deliberately removed, respect for those less forceful is present and we solicit the timid voice. More often than not, the timid voice will spring to life and introduce a wealth of experience and insight to the conversation. A skillful listener actively solicits ideas and opinions from those with timid voices. Those ideas and opinions often turn out to be surprisingly useful to speaker and listener alike!

Practice: *Identify a friend or acquaintance who is normally quiet and reserved in group settings. Next time you're together in a group,*

*see what creative possibilities you can come
up with to encourage that person to be more
self-expressive.*

30. Listen for inconsistencies

How many times have you had the experience of hearing someone speak and their
words simply do not ring true? Inconsistencies are mismatches and they frequently occur
between what a person says – the content of
their communication – and the feeling tone
behind the words. Daily communication often
contains such incongruities. "No problem!"
and "I'm so sorry" can often mean the exact
opposite if someone is speaking
unconsciously or insincerely.

In addition to voice tone, body language
can also contradict spoken words. A person
proclaiming themselves to be happy while
sitting slumped with a frown on their face
sends a mixed message. Likewise, a person
who laughs nervously as a defense in emotionally loaded circumstances is demonstra-
ting incongruous or inconsistent communication.

A skillful listener learns to recognize inconsistencies. They listen for the feeling that is expressed even when the words don't match the communication. The feelings communicated through the mixed message will be the more accurate and truthful aspect of the communication. When two feelings seem to be at odds, whatever appears to be most appropriate to the situation will be the one to pay close attention to. The trick in addressing inconsistencies, as in much that constitutes skillful listening, is to respond in compassionate ways that do not reinforce or increase defensiveness.

Practice: *Next time you're at a party or meeting, spend time listening and watching for mismatches between what someone is saying, and their facial expressions and body postures. Which feels like the more authentic communication?*

31. Listen with a soft belly

When we listen to others whose viewpoints differ from ours, or to people who say things we feel we must defend against, we often tense up and feel irritated or frustrated. Repeated occurrences of this type of stress are unhealthy. How then, can we listen to what is difficult to hear, without too much wear and tear on us?

Skillful listeners listen with a "soft belly." Dr. Daniel Levitin, author of *The Organized Mind*, teaches positive emotion refocusing as one way to calm down the physical response to anger and frustration.[8] When you feel yourself getting upset in a conversation, breathe in a few deep, slow breaths all the way down into your belly enough to push it out. Then relax your belly and let it go completely soft. Slowly exhale. After a few deep breaths, bring the image of someone you love or a scene from nature that makes you feel peaceful into your mind's eye. Imagine this scene or person centered in your heart area. Keep breathing slow, deep breaths and ask the peaceful part of you that holds the image, what you can do to resolve the problem at hand.

When we allow our bodies to quiet down during a conversation that disturbs us, we are most open to positive solutions. We tend less to create an "enemy image" of the speaker, or harbor deep-seated grudges against another.

Practice: *Think of something that triggers an emotional reaction in you. Breathe slowly into your chest. Now move the breath into the middle of your belly. Continue to breathe slowly and deeply. Do this for a few breaths then return to the thought or image that you originally found upsetting. Has the anger been reduced or softened? Practice moving the breath from the chest to the belly the next time you feel irritated or tense in a meeting or conversation.*

32. Return to the present moment's needs

For many of us, much of everyday life isn't lived in the present moment. Instead, we live in what neurologist Robert Scaer calls, "dissociative capsules" resulting from large and small traumas.[9] Very little of what we talk about every day deals with in-the-moment current events, needs, or wants. One of the great gifts a skillful listener brings to the table can be a reminder that our lives unfold and take place in the here and now. One way a skillful listener can help a speaker reclaim the present moment is to inquire about thoughts and feelings as they are occurring. "What does that feel like?" "What do you want right now?" "Is there something you need now that I can help with?" These and other responses lead the focus back to the present moment. Such responses help us practice mindfulness.

The benefit of a present-moment focus is the central theme in Eckhart Tolle's book, *The Power of Now*.[10] In the present moment is where everything that we want and need is rooted, and helping to facilitate that awareness and recognition is of inestimable value.

Practice: *Pay close attention to how things feel to you in this moment – in your body and in your mind. Are you thirsty? Hungry? Sad? Happy? Feel a need to get up and move? See how many times in a day you can take a present-moment "break!" Paying attention to such things is actually skillful self-listening.*

33. Develop methods for skillful self-listening

Skilled listeners are able to listen deeply to themselves. They ask: "What's true for me? What do I want? What can I do to obtain what I want?"

A well-known adage instructs, "If you bring forth what is inside you, it will save you. If you do not bring forth what is inside you, it will destroy you."[11] Listening is one primary way that we discover the riches that live deep within us.

Another simple and direct way to listen to oneself is to begin a process of discerning an *ordo amorum* (the priority of things we love) for oneself. Who am I? What do I love? What do I love most?

Two all-encompassing self-questions that researchers have found to be enormouslypowerful when asked over and over again are the very ones at the top of this page: *What's true for me?* and *What do I want?*[12] Asking these two questions repeatedly will not only help to crystallize wishes, wants, and dreams, but will also help to reinvigorate and re-inspire efforts that may have been temporarily halted due to any number of life's pressing distractions and concerns.

Practice: Spend a month writing a double-entry journal. First, ask and write answers to the two questions above: What's true for me? What do I want? Then come back at the end of a month and write commentary on the entries that you have made the previous month. What common themes emerge? Can you see how this might be a means of profound self-listening?
(http://www.sdcoe.k12.ca.us/SCORE/actbank/tdentry.htm)

34. Cultivate patience

Patience is a learned skill and as such, has to be practiced. Skillful listeners are patience practitioners. Those who have accomplished some measure of proficiency in being patient, share an understanding that hearing someone out – helping them get to the heart of the matter – takes time. And it's that time they're willing to offer.

Skillful listeners possess a ready willingness to *temporarily* suspend whatever needs for self-expression they may have, while they focus on others without any great need for them to be succinct, speedy or clear in what they have to say. They are not disturbed when a speaker, who is working through a significant issue, rambles or repeats the same story over and over again in different ways. Skillful, patient listeners carry *Beginner's Ear* (Skill No. 8) with them, often letting them hear the same story as if hearing it for the first time.

How exactly does someone go about cultivating patience? With practice and a clear understanding of the benefits that patience offers to oneself and others. And by knowing and understanding that others need to tell their stories to someone who cares, and that there is a freeing, healing value inherent in such telling.

Practice: Experiment with three things that might work to help you be more patient with yourself and those around you. Whatever works for you to become more patient is worth discovering and practicing. It is a sign that you have temporarily put aside your own ego needs in service to another. Patience is love in action.

35. Become someone who can hear hard truths

There are many direct ways we let others know we don't want to hear hard truths that will upset us. We might say, "I don't want to hear that," "Let's not go there," or "I don't want to talk about problems, only solutions." We also have indirect ways we let people know what not to tell us. A common way is to express anger or frustration in response to things people say that we don't like. These are often people we have the closest relation-ships with – coworkers, intimates, children, parents, etc.

Listening to hard truths stretches us to open our hearts and minds to topics that are emotionally charged for us. They challenge us to be slow to anger, disagree or criticize (Skill No. 6). But being slow with those negative responses is exactly what we must do if we want someone to trust us enough to share even their easy truths with us.

What must we do if we truly want to become someone to whom hard truths can be readily told? We must find *authentic* ways to value, praise and honor such truth-tellers. We must develop increasing capacity to recognize the gifts such messengers bring us, even when their message might initially feel painful and threatening. James Bishop understood both the power and the difficulty in being able to hear hard truths: "The truth which makes us free is for the most part, the truth which we prefer not to hear."[13]

Practice: *Pay attention when someone close to you stops short of telling you something difficult. Notice what you may be doing to close down the conversation. What might you do to make it safe to reopen again?*

36. Be mindful of age, race and gender bias

When we listen to someone, we subconsciously filter what they are saying through biases of age, race and gender. If you are a woman, it may be easier to hear what another woman has to say. If you are a person of color, it may be easier to hear another person of color. We generally listen better to people who are close to us in age, race and gender. Neuroscientists consider that these are learned behaviors with a neurological basis.[14]

But skillful listeners are mindful of such biases. They bring their unconscious biases into the light of day and examine exactly how they listen to both genders, various age groups and different races, and they correct any deficits in their listening accordingly. All human beings deserve our skillful listening. We listen better when we listen to the heart of the person speaking, as opposed to their age, race, or gender.

Practice: This week spend time noticing if you change your listening habits and skills when you listen to men versus women. What things change when you listen to people of different races, ages and genders? What three things do you need to do in order to be more mindful of age, race and gender?

37. Break the "I" habit

Many years ago, before privacy laws were enacted, the New York Telephone Company listened in on phone conversations as part of a research project to discover the most frequently used words in conversations. The number one word was "I."

Most of us don't realize how much of our daily talk is about ourselves. It's a habit we began as children – one we've found little reason to change. Here are a few good reasons to break that habit: the word "I" stifles true dialogue as well as the opportunity to learn anything new about the person you are in a conversation with, or a subject that they may know something about that you don't. "I" stifles creative partnerships, teamwork and discovering new ways to fulfill others needs.

When we ask more questions about others, and discuss with them the content of their conversation using the word "you" (as long as we're not bossing or blaming), a new world opens up. Others will be attracted to us and we will win a new level of respect.

Skilled listeners are aware of the benefits of using the word "you" more often than "I."

Practice: *For the next seven days, refrain from beginning a sentence with "I." Be aware of how many times you refer to yourself in a conversation. As you use the word "I" less and less, notice how people respond to you.*

38. Ask specific, clarifying questions

We often assume we understand what a person means by the words they use and their generally agreed upon meaning. However, consider this: as mentioned earlier, each of the 800 words that we regularly and repeatedly use in everyday English has an average of seventeen different definitions![15] Other languages have similar limitations. Is it any wonder that we are so frequently surprised to discover that what we thought someone meant, after close questioning, we then discover they meant something else entirely?

A skillful listener knows that meaning is tricky and subjective. When we engage in dialogue, we frequently speak thoughts off the top of our heads. First thoughts work like first drafts in writing – they require a good editor/listener to clarify meaning and intent. Like a writer attempting to commit a vision to the page, a speaker may have trouble finding and using words to express all that he or she may be thinking and feeling. Asking specific, clarifying questions can frequently help bring a speaker's subject into clear focus.

How do we know when something needs clarification? One way is to tune our ears for certain words that signal unclear generalizations. Words like "they," "everyone," "always," "never," or "nobody" are a few examples. When asked to clarify or elaborate, such generalizations often end up referring to specific people, places, times and things. It is a generous act of service to bring about this kind of realization.

Practice: *Listen for generalizations and globalizations in your next several conversations. They often show up in the words described above. See if you can get the speaker to become more specific in their speech.*

39. Say what's useful; say what's true

Some people can't wait to "get things off their chest" or "give someone a piece of their mind." They take great pride in "not pulling any punches" and in "telling it like it is." However, this style of communication has a certain kind of egocentric aggressiveness in it. Skillful listeners do not respond in this way.

Skillful listeners respond with what they know to be factual, true, and beneficial to others. Skillful listeners also develop a sense of timeliness – recognizing the "right" moment for saying such things. In other words, out of a sense of genuine affection and care for others, a thoughtful and skillful listener realizes that an important element of truth-telling involves understanding exactly what another person is able and ready to hear. In addition to what is truthful, they consider what will be most useful to another.

The distinction between the skillful style and the egocentric style is simple and easy to distinguish: one is thoughtful and other-centered, and the other is thoughtless and self-centered, caring little about the real needs and wishes of another.

How do we best determine what someone might be ready, willing and able to hear? If someone is feeling defensive and hurt, they are unlikely to be able to usefully receive "truth-telling." One excellent way to find out what a person is ready to hear and find useful is simply ... to ask them!

Practice: *Think of someone that you'd like to "give a piece of your mind" to. What is your motivation for such action? If you could transform your intention or motivation, how might you speak so that what you have to say could be heard and put to good use?*

Section Three Reflection Questions

What does it feel like when I listen deeply to someone?

What have I heard recently that I may have found disturbing? How did I respond?

What have I noticed about my capacity to pay ever closer attention?

Notes to myself...

"All things, animate and inanimate, have within them, a spirit dimension. They communicate in that dimension to those who can listen."

~ Jerome Bernstein
Jungian Analyst

"Sit down here and tell me about it."

The train clanked and rattled through the suburbs of Tokyo on a drowsy spring afternoon. Our car was comparatively empty – a few housewives with their kids in tow, some old folks going shopping. I gazed absently at the drab houses and dusty hedgerows.

At one station the doors opened, and suddenly the afternoon quiet was shattered by a man bellowing violent, incomprehensible curses. The man staggered into our car. He wore laborer's clothing, and he was big, drunk, and dirty. Screaming, he swung at a woman holding a baby. The blow sent her spinning into the laps of an elderly couple. It was a miracle that the baby was unharmed.

Terrified, the couple jumped up and scrambled toward the other end of the car. The laborer aimed a kick at the retreating back of the old woman but missed as she scuttled to safety. This so enraged the drunk that he grabbed the metal pole in the center of the car and tried to wrench it out of its stanchion. I could see that one of his hands was cut and bleeding. The train lurched ahead, the passengers frozen with fear. I stood up.

I was young then, some twenty years ago, and in pretty good shape. I'd been putting in a solid eight hours of aikido training nearly every day for the past three years. I liked to throw and grapple. I thought I was tough. The trouble was, my martial skill was untested in actual combat. As students of aikido, we were not allowed to fight.

"Aikido," my teacher had said again and again, "is the art of reconciliation. Whoever has the mind to fight has broken his connection with the universe. If you try to dominate people, you are already defeated. We study how to resolve conflict, not how to start it."

I listened to his words. I tried hard. I even went so far as to cross the street to avoid the *chimpira*, the pinball punks who lounged around the train stations. My forbearance exalted me. I felt both tough and holy. In my heart, however, I wanted an absolutely legitimate opportunity whereby I might save the innocent by destroying the guilty.

"This is it!" I said to myself as I got to my feet. "People are in danger. If I don't do something fast, somebody will probably get hurt."

Seeing me stand up, the drunk recognized a chance to focus his rage. "Aha!" he roared. "A foreigner! You need a lesson in Japanese manners!"

I held on lightly to the commuter strap overhead and gave him a slow look of disgust and dismissal. I planned to take this turkey apart, but he had to make the first move. I wanted him mad, so I pursed my lips and blew him an insolent kiss.

"All right!" he hollered. "You're gonna get a lesson in Japanese manners." He gathered himself for a rush at me.

A fraction of a second before he could move, someone shouted "Hey!" It was ear-splitting. I remember the strangely joyous, lilting quality of it – as though you and a friend had been searching diligently for something, and he had suddenly stumbled upon it. "Hey!"

I wheeled to my left; the drunk spun to his right. We both stared down at a little, old

Japanese man. He must have been well into his seventies, this tiny gentleman, sitting there immaculate in his kimono. He took no notice of me, but beamed delightedly at the laborer, as though he had a most important, most welcome secret to share.

"C'mere," the old man said in an easy vernacular, beckoning to the drunk. "C'mere and talk with me." He waved his hand lightly.

The big man followed, as if on a string. He planted his feet belligerently in front of the old gentleman, and roared above the clacking wheels, "Why the hell should I talk to you?"

The drunk now had his back to me. If his elbow moved so much as a millimeter, I'd drop him in his socks.

The old man continued to beam at the laborer. "What'cha been drinkin'?' he asked, his eyes sparkling with interest.

"I been drinkin' sake," the laborer bellowed back, "and it's none of your business!" Flecks of spittle spattered the old man.

"Oh, that's wonderful," the old man said, "absolutely wonderful! You see, I love sake, too. Every night, me and my wife – she's seventy-six, you know – we warm up a little bottle of sake and take it out into the garden, and we sit on an old wooden bench. We watch the sun go down, and we look to see how our persimmon tree is doing. My great-grand-father planted that tree, and we worry about whether it will recover from those ice storms we had last winter. Our tree has done better than I expected, though, especially when you consider the poor quality of the soil. It's gratifying to watch when we take our sake and go out to enjoy the evening - even when it rains!" He looked up at the laborer, eyes twinkling.

As he struggled to follow the old man's conversation, the drunk's face began to soften. His fists slowly unclenched. "Yeah," he said. "I love persimmons, too. . . ." His voice trailed off.

"Yes," said the old man, smiling, "and I'm sure you have a wonderful wife."

"No," replied the laborer. "My wife died."

Very gently, swaying with the motion of the train, the big man began to sob. "I don't got no wife. I don't got no home. I don't got no job. I'm so ashamed of myself." Tears rolled down his cheeks; a spasm of despair rippled through his body.

Now it was my turn. Standing there in my well-scrubbed youthful innocence, my make-this-world-safe-for-democracy righteousness, I suddenly felt dirtier than he was.

Then the train arrived at my stop. As the doors opened, I heard the old man cluck sympathetically. "My, my," he said, "That is a difficult predicament, indeed. Sit down here and tell me about it."

I turned my head for one last look. The laborer was sprawled on the seat, his head in the old man's lap. The old man was softly stroking the filthy, matted hair. As the train pulled away, I sat down on a bench. What I had wanted to do with muscle...had been accomplished with love.

~ Terry Dobson

40. Say what you see

Jiddu Krishnamurti, the respected wisdom teacher famous for asserting that "truth is a pathless land," recognized that to interact with people in a variety of everyday situations without making evaluations of any sort, by "saying what you see" clearly, demonstrates a high level of intelligence and discernment.[16]

When we say what we see, we take our cues from what is present right in front of us. We follow rather than lead. We go where others are willing and ready to take us. We don't interpret. If a speaker is frowning, a skilled listener says, "I see you are frowning." It is much more helpful than offering an interpretation, such as: "I see you are angry," or "Why are you sad?"

By saying what we see, we also avoid making comparisons or being judgmental. "I see clothes on the floor" can be a simple statement of observation, without having to carry the judgment: "You are messy."

One central problem with language is that much of it is based on evaluation, interpretation and comparison. It is a great challenge to find things to say that are *not* interpretations or comparisons. Saying what we see compassionately offers the speaker the opportunity to show and tell us how they see things. It creates the opportunity for us to help a speaker go deeper into their experience, and possibly reach "hard truths" they may want and need to share (Skill No. 35).

Practice: Look around you. Pick a series of things that you can readily see. Silently say what they are. Notice where judgment wants to enter in. "I see a messy room" is a different statement than the intended neutral assessment, "I see clothes on the floor. There are books on the bed. A pair of shoes is on the chair."

41. Use intention clarification

Oftentimes in the heat of a passionate discussion, we may sometimes find ourselves at a loss for words. We don't know what to say next. We need some space and a few moments to regroup and gather our thoughts, to reconnect with so-called "executive prefrontal brain function." At these times, it's good to have a few "space-making" tools that we can deploy as necessary.

One such tool is to ask directly what a person's intention is with their communication. They might not immediately know what their intention is, but often, after considering it for a few moments, many people will be able to tell you:

"I want you to know how painful this afternoon's argument was for me."

"I'm frustrated trying to find the words to describe this morning's meeting."

"What you're doing with the family's finances frightens me, and I want you to know I intend to be more involved."

Inquiring about a person's intention works remarkably well to get both speaker and listener aligned and back on track. As the speaker comes up with a clarifying response, the listener gains some time to gather their thoughts and offer an appropriate response that will further the discussion in a positive way, rather than shut it down or divert it. Such an intervention can serve as a springboard to even further explorations.

Practice: *Next time you find yourself in an emotionally intense interaction, remember to pause at some point and simply ask: "What's your intention with what you're saying?"*

42. Maximize the listening environment

The physical environment where listening takes place can significantly affect the experience either negatively or positively. There are many venues where speaking and listening to one another is actually inappropriate and would negatively affect a listener's ability. Some common examples would be trying to have a conversation during a movie, in a library, at a music recital, sporting event, or during a memorial service or a wedding.

Distractions also diminish the listening experience. For example, interruptions from cell phones or other attention distracters like TVs and radios can hinder the listening experience. Noble listeners avoid unnecessary distractions.

Skilled listeners also work to maximize the listening environment when they are clear about the purpose of the conversation and the time limits available. Maximizing the listening environment is so important that a skilled listener will put off a conversation that cannot be held in a place where listening can flourish.

Practice: *Identify half a dozen things that you can think of that go into making up an ideal listening environment for you. They might include things like time of day (some people listen better in the morning; others in the afternoon or evening), physical space, indoors or out, time constraints and distractions you can avoid (for example, turn off your cell phone), etc.*

43. Learn to listen to your own lacunae

The ways we are raised and the experiences we have as children significantly shape the way we see the world and behave as adults, especially in the first three years. We learn to pay attention to certain things and filter out others. The result is that spaces or gaps form in our knowledge and perceptions that govern our daily life experience. Known as *lacunae* in the medical literature, these spaces in our neurological network operate as a kind of filtering system when it comes to seeing, listening, or speaking. Some of the things that work as powerful filters are painful childhood memories, strong family beliefs, unexamined assumptions, personal prejudices, and unconscious expectations.

Many of us operate with awareness of these filters only when some glaring omission, error or oversight makes them so obvious that we can no longer deny them. For example, a belief that people who aren't able to sit in traditional postures for formal meditation practice are somehow deficient might stand in stark relief when the direct experience of time spent with such people brings great satisfaction.

The first thing for a skillful listener to do about their lacunae or filters is to recognize that they exist in each of us. Dispelling ignorance of them allows us to be curious and provides the possibility for exploration and examination. This self-awareness then allows us to be more open and compassionate to others as well as to our own shortcomings.

Practice: *Based upon things that you find yourself forgetting or repeatedly overlooking, begin to notice what some of your own psychological "holes" might be. Consider designing a plan or practice for effectively working with and integrating them.*

44. Practice Strategic Questioning

Strategic questions have a number of elements that make them unique and set them apart from run-of-the-mill, everyday questions. Developed by San Francisco-based activist Fran Peavey, Strategic Questions are asked with the intention to reveal ambiguity and open up fresh options for exploration.

They can be tough questions because they break through the façade of false confidence and reveal the profound uncertainty that underlies all reality. Nevertheless, they also invite movement toward growth and new possibilities. Strategic Questions empower people to create strategies for change in many areas of life.

There are eight key features that distinguish a Strategic Question. First, a Strategic Question is a helpful, dynamic challenge that encourages movement and change. Instead of "Where should I apply for a job?" a Strategic Question might ask, "What work would I be happy doing for the rest of my life?"

A Strategic Question encourages options. Instead of "Who might we get to help us with this project?" a more dynamic possibility might be: "Which people can we support and ally with to help build co-operative synergies?"

A third feature of Strategic Questions is that they are empowering. Examples often begin with the query, "What would it take …?" For example, "What would it take to make you feel your life had ever-expanding purpose and meaning?"

Two more features of Strategic Questions are that they don't ask "Why?" and they cannot be answered "Yes" or "No." Questions that ask "Why?" close down creative options and often generate guilt and defensiveness.

Questions that can be answered "Yes" or "No" often only skim the surface or bring dialogue and inquiry to a dead end.

Next, Strategic Questions address taboo topics. There is tremendous power to create change inherent in them, because they challenge underlying values and assumptions. An example of such a question would be "What was it that kept us from talking about our teacher's cancer for so long?"

A seventh aspect of Strategic Questions is that they tend to be simply structured, focusing on one thing at a time. "What one thing can you do to make your work more enjoyable?" or "What will restore the vitality in your spiritual practice?"

Finally, Strategic Questions assume human equality. They are deeply respectful of people and their capacity to change and grow in healthy ways. They are positive, life-affirming inquiries designed and intended to support human personal, professional and spiritual transformation.

Practice: *Spend a week asking different people Strategic Questions based on one of* *the eight characteristics. See how much depth comes out of the questions. For deepening your understanding of yourself, spend some time creating Strategic Questions about your own life. If you really want to dig deep, write 25 Strategic Questions about listening itself and see if you can live your way into the answers. Be forewarned, your life will change in profound ways!*

45. The ears can be ready when the heart's just not

All of us have discussion topics that generate great fear and anxiety for us. In his book, *Magical Child*, Joseph Pearce recognized: "Anxiety is the enemy of intelligence," and those things that we can't face or speak about directly, have great power over our lives, whether we're aware of it or not.[17]

These taboo topics are often guilt or shame-based – some unfortunate incident from our past that lives buried in the depths of our psyche. They live in us like live wires, and anytime such topics are raised, they set off a great charge of large emotional energy.

This is the experience of being limbically hijacked – irrationally reactive – and many find the experience painful and surprising to both themselves and to others. Such reactivity is often connected with loss, or fear, or some other early trauma, sometimes pre-verbal.

As with much that has to do with skillful listening, the first step in dealing with taboo topics is to become aware that "talking about X, for some reason makes me very uncomfortable." Money, success, sex, loss and death head up many people's lists. But the specific topics are really secondary. What's primary for a skillful listener to know is that our pre-existing uneasiness is triggered by such topics, and that people who raise them up for discussion are most likely not trying to deliberately cause us pain. Nevertheless, taboo topics can be a stumbling block to hearing others' hard truths (Skill No. 35).

Practice: *Over the next week, find someone with whom you share trust and ask them to talk about a topic that feels taboo or unsettling. Death, love, sex, and money are good trigger topics. Notice how it feels when*

the ears are ready to hear but the heart is not.
How can you hold your heart open to fully
hear what the speaker is saying?

46. Don't blame the victim

It is all too common in many cultures to place responsibility for violations of respect and dignity on the people who have suffered. We blame the victim. It is human to feel that the victims are responsible in some way. It puts such problems "out there," and helps protect us from anxiety about becoming victims ourselves. Blaming the victim can make us feel more powerful and more in control of our lives. Clearly, we reason, we are smarter, stronger, healthier, luckier, and have our lives more together, so nothing like what happened to them could ever happen to us. Blaming the victim is one way to avoid feeling powerless when someone's life is in crisis.

Listening to victims and victim stories takes practice and skill. It's easy to inadvertently and unwittingly slip into a blaming-the-victim stance. People who have suffered seriously in their lives often need to tell their story over and over, in order to come to some healing resolution. A skillful listener listens with fresh ears every time, curious and open to the possibility that this will be the occasion when resolution happens, that a victim will find a true opening to the possibility of healing and ultimately, forgiveness.

Practice: *The next time you speak to someone going through a difficult time who has already told you their story, be willing to hear it again, to listen deeply with open ears, mind and heart. See if you can hear something new, all the while trusting that, as the Truth and Reconciliation story prefacing second section in this book demonstrates, listening is often all that is required for healing to unfold.*

47. Recognize your own "exit strategies"

In addition to "anxiety being the enemy of intelligence," it is also responsible for all of our "exit strategies." Exit strategies are the things we do to turn away from situations that make us anxious. Anxiety and exit strategies, if not skillfully attended to, work against skillful listening.

Exit strategies can take almost any form: daydreaming, pill-popping, drinking coffee or alcohol, watching TV, eating sweets, smoking – the list is endless. Anything that we move towards in an attempt to eradicate or reduce anxiety can serve as a positive or a negative exit strategy.

Learning to identify, recognize and re-spond positively to such exit strategies can serve several purposes. First of all, it helps us to recognize when we're feeling anxious. Many of us rarely know – we turn towards our exit strategies before we are at all consciously aware of our anxiety. A skilled listener learns about their exit strategies and learns to over-come the anxiety or fear that creates them.

Another reason to pay attention to exit strategies is that we can acquire and begin to secure options to deal with our anxieties. Instead of going off to grab a beer, we can consider hanging in, exploring what's true for us, and asking for what we want instead. We can begin to skillfully listen to ourselves as we listen more skillfully to others.

Practice: *Pay close attention the next time you feel anxious. Be curious about what anxiety feels like in your mind and body. Is it a tension in your stomach or lower back? A constriction in your chest or throat? A pain in your neck? By learning to recognize anxiety's telltale sensations in our body, we can then do things to address it directly.*

48. Practice the power of attunement

Attunement is one of the most powerful forces on the planet. It begins as resonance in the mother's womb when the baby first begins attuning to the mother's voice. It continues throughout life in our intimate relationships or with colleagues and friends. It is the feeling of being "at one" with another.

Attunement is not the same as agreement. One can be attuned to another and respectfully disagree. With skillful listening, we can listen and not judge and take in what the other is saying, but not necessarily agree. Our body recognizes when we are in attunement and it feels good!

From recent neuroscience research, we know that attunement also feels good in the brain. A brain under stress becomes unorganized and attunement helps soothe and organize it.[18]

Practice: *When you listen to someone today, imagine yourself as an instrument in an orchestra. Allow the speaker to play the notes he or she must play and do not judge or try to change the music. Allow your own music to play, with the intention of making beautiful music together.*

49. Practice taking crap

In *Seeking Enlightenment Hat By Hat*, writer Nevada Barr tells of working in law enforcement.[19] One day a grizzled old veteran let her in on a little secret: the real job of a peace officer is to "take crap" he told her. However, he neglected to offer her many skillful ways to actually go about doing that.

When someone is sending negative, "stinky" energy in our direction – anger, criticism, or complaints – it is can sometimes feel as if they are hurling pointed barbs in our direction. Never remain seated or standing directly in front of such energy. In order to continue skillfully listening without suffering harm, stand up, walk back and forth in front of the person, or walk alongside. Keep yourself out of the direct line of their communication. A moving target is much harder to hit, and physical movement helps regulate adrenaline and cortisol, the primary stress chemicals in the body.

For the most part, the speaker in such a state will not even notice, and moving serves as a disciplined way to fill in the gap between hearing and reacting negatively in return. This is contrary to the way we have been taught to deal with disturbing people and situations. Mostly we're taught to simply sit and take it, or to throw the "crap" right back. But moving or "dancing" with a disturbing situation, rather than simply "taking it," is an extremely useful and worthwhile personal practice.

Practice: Next time you're in an emotionally charged exchange with someone, remember to get up and move. Stand and pace or walk side by side in close proximity. See how it affects what you hear the speaker saying and subsequently, your ability to be non-reactive with them.

50. Learn to say "No"

Saying "No" can be very difficult. Often we think we have to meet the expectations of others. It can sometimes be a challenging, anxiety-filled act to set limits. But when we do things against our will or against our own needs at the time, we can end up feeling used and resentful. A simple and direct "No, I am not able to listen to you right now" is often the best solution.

If someone requests us to listen, it's fair to ask for time to think it over. We can do so and get back to them later. Do we really want to listen? If not, then "No" is the honest answer. We can use an empathic "No" if we find ourselves listening to things that are attacking or harmful. It is not until we can actually, honestly and easily say "No," that our "Yes" begins to truly mean "Yes" and our "No" begins to truly mean "No."

Here are five different ways to say "No." 1. The direct "No": "No" means "No"; 2. The reflecting "No": we acknowledge the content and feeling of the request, then add the assertive refusal at the end; 3. The reasoned "No": we give a brief and genuine reason for the refusal without opening up further negotiation; 4. The rain check "No": A way of saying "No" to a specific request without giving a definite "No"; 5. The broken record: Repeat the simple statement of refusal again and again. It's often necessary to use this with persistent requests, especially from children.

Practice: *Pay attention to times when you say "Yes" and later realize you really wish you had said "No." Find some compassionate way to go back and offer a "retroactive No." In other words, just because we've said "Yes" initially, doesn't mean we can't say "No" later, and say "No" the next time if feels right to do so. Becoming a skilled listener does not*

mean you have to listen to everyone and
everything all the time.

51. Watch for compassion fatigue

The world is filled with pain and suffering – the First Noble Truth has a reality basis to it. None of us gets through life without a handful of heartaches or traumatic experiences.

Sometimes, listening to the pain and suffering of others can cause us to close off our hearts. And a closed heart can't love as fully or listen as deeply as an open heart.

What is one to do when there is so much pain in the world and the heart is so vulnerable? How does one listen and not fall victim to compassion fatigue? One way is to make it a point balance seeing the beauty around us that is as equally abundant as the pain and suffering. By breathing in the beauty of mother earth and the mystery of creation, we take time for renewal, time required to sustain us in listening to others' pain. Practicing gratitude is one more good way to keep a heart open and ready to reach out to listen and love and to receive the love and grace from others.

For it's not so much the ears we use to hear with, as it is our hearts.

Practice: *Find the gift, the abundance, the beauty in the world around you this very minute. Look at the clouds, the sun, or the rain, or the birds outside your window. Remember that you are part of an incredible creation beyond our comprehension. Breathe in a belly full of that mystery and grace.*

52. Create a community of practice

Most of us like doing things together with people who like doing things with us. When several people come together and agree to collaborate and support each other's growing and learning, extraordinary possibilities begin to emerge.

Learning and practice are infinitely more fun and results are more easily accomplished when we do it with others, when we organize what's known as a "community of practice." Ask friends, family, colleagues, or members of your church, temple or sangha to practice with you. Small, faith-based groups have been quite effective in helping each other learn to listen skillfully, and workplace listening groups can help transform people as well as productivity.

As we work with others learning to be skilled listeners, great understanding for the difficult and unending details of the work result.[22] There is an understanding of the struggles required to meet the challenges of becoming a skillful listener in a world that mostly celebrates talkers. An expanding community of skillful listeners practicing together has the power to positively transform everyone involved.

Practice: Ask a few of your friends, family, or colleagues to buy this or some similar book and create a "Listening Club" dedicated to helping each other learn to become a skillful listener. You can meet every week for a year and discuss and practice one skill at a time, or create your own time-line. Faith-based groups have found working collect- with this book helps them live the Golden Rule on a daily basis.

Section Four Reflection Questions

Which areas of my life have been positively transformed by practicing the skills in this book?

Who do I think would benefit from receiving a copy of this book?

Who can I ask to join me in a Community of Practice in learning to be a more skilled listener?

Notes to myself...

Conclusion

The power of practice

The transformation into a skilled listener is an emotionally and spiritually challenging endeavor. Many feelings and new realizations arise as we attempt to learn about others and ourselves. It is a challenge well worth turning toward. The ongoing practice of listening transforms not only the speaker with its healing attention and compassionate focus, but it transforms the listener as well. With practice, listeners grow bigger hearts, greater neural integration, and have more compassion, wisdom and solutions for successfully navigating life's challenges.

Skilled listeners lead lives that are more peaceful and successful. There is no other skill on the planet that has the power to positively change so many people with so little investment of time and energy – the time put into practice. As David Augsburger so eloquently told us in the beginning of this book: "Being listened is so close to being loved that most people don't know the difference." In practicing how to skillfully listen, you spread that form of love and peace throughout a world that sorely needs it. The power is in the practice.

The power of attunement

Attunement is one of the most powerful forces on earth. It starts in the mother's womb and ideally continues all through life.

Unfortunately attunement occurs less often than it might, as many people do not know how best to actually attune to others. Skillful listening is an extraordinary way to move into attunement. You can practice and learn what it sounds like and what it feels like in the mind and body. Attunement heals.[20]

The power of the sangha

It is my deepest desire to create a global community of skilled listeners – to teach people how to use listening as a spiritual practice to connect in ways that benefit everyone. We know from recent research that positive interpersonal connections grow body, mind and soul.[21] Groups of people working together at becoming skillful listeners – a sangha - create a more mindful, peaceful, understanding, creative, cooperative world. I invite you to join me in this endeavor.

The Life Events Impact History

Mark Brady, Ph.D. &
Jennifer Austin Leigh, Psy.D.

Instructions:

1. Place a check mark next to any phrase that describes an event that happened at any time in your life.

2. Place the letter "R" next to any phrase that describes an event that occurred more than once in your life (Repeated).

3. Place the letter "S" next to any phrase that describes an event that happened that caused you to feel over-whelmed, helpless, terrified, rage-filled or frozen (Shock).

Harm by commission
(Hurts by others):

Physical, sexual verbal or emotional abuse

Disrespectful treatment (e.g. insults, lies)

Punitive discipline

Valued for achievements – not who you are

Unreasonably high adult expectations

Ignoring or rejecting of painful emotions

Love or attention conditional on your good behavior

Racism, sexism

Over-control by caretakers

Harm by omission (Unmet needs):

Physical or emotional neglect

Insufficient nurturing contact, holding or nonsexual touch

Lack of opportunities to form attachments

Lack of
stimulation

Lack of autonomy

Unfulfilled
promises

Situational harm
(Caused by life
circumstances;
indirect):

Prenatal or birth
trauma

Illnesses, injuries,
medical
procedures or
surgeries

Subjected to
general anesthesia
or IV sedation

Lack of
communication

Left out of school
activities

Important events
unacknowledged

Loss of
attachments
(separation or
death)

Short separation
(depends on age)

Over-stimulation

Developmental
frustrations and
fears

Inescapable
restraints

Major changes
(e.g. new sibling,
home, or school)

Primary caretaker
dysfunction
(e.g.anxiety, grief,
anger, illness)

Primary caretaker
disputes,
separation or
divorce

Primary caretaker
alcoholism or
drug abuse

Dysfunctional
nuclear or
extended family
system

Natural disasters
(e.g. fires, floods,
earthquakes,
tornadoes,
hurricanes)

Exposure to
violence (through
real life or the
media)

Other frightening
events

Disappointments
or unforeseen
occurrences

Arguments with
caretakers, peers
or siblings

Adapted from:
> *Tears and Tantrums* by Aletha J. Solter, Shining Star Press, 1998.

Scoring:

If you indicated more than two or three items with an "R" or an "S" there is a high probability that you have been exposed to repeated or one-time shock trauma experiences. These experiences very likely have had a significant impact on your life in the past and may continue to impact your life today. Such experiences live in the brain as physically encapsulated groups of neurons, and in the body as residual "energy cysts." They interfere with our ability to listen skillfully to another as they distort our version of reality and close our heart to a great deal of love and acceptance. We untangle the present by unraveling the knots of the past, and so being listened to with care and compassion is a first step in beginning to clear the body of these residual experiences. On the following page is a list of resources from recent neuropsychology and traumatology research that the astute reader is encouraged to investigate further.

Healing Resources ~~

David Baldwin's Trauma Information Center
http://www.trauma-pages.com

Peter Levine's Foundation for Human
Enrichment
http://www.traumahealing.com

Bessel van der Kolk's Boston Trauma Center
http://www.traumacenter.org

Ron Kurtz's Hakomi Institute
http://www.hakomiinstitute.com/main.htm

Francine Shapiro's EMDR Institute
http://www.emdr.com/shapiro.htm

Pat Ogden's Sensorimotor Institute
http://sensorimotorpsychotherapy.org/
faculty.html

John Fox's Institute of Poetic Medicine
http://www.poeticmedicine.com

Damasio, Antonio (1999). *The Feeling of What Happens: Body and Emotion in the Making of Consciousness.* NY: Harcourt Brace & Company

Levitin, D. (2014). *The organized mind: Thinking straight in the age of information overload.* NY: Dutton.

Rothchild, Babette (2000). *The Body Remembers: The Psychophysiology of Trauma and Trauma Treatment* NY: WW Norton

van der Kolk, B. (2014). *The body keeps the score.* NY: Viking Press.

A Listening Manifesto

I believe I have the power and potential to change my life and create more love and peace in the world.

I believe listening is one key to attuning with others to   create magnificent relationships at home, work, church, temple, and play.

I believe listening is a learnable and teachable skill.

I believe that others can learn to listen and attune.

I believe others want to speak and be deeply heard, and they want to learn to deeply listen.

I believe I have an open heart that will grow only larger and more open as I learn to listen.

I believe the most abundant harvests in my relationships are yet to come as I learn to listen.

I believe as I change my life through listening I will be rewarded in my relationships and work.

I believe by using my listening skills I will be more fulfilled, happier and successful in life.

I believe that working with others to learn skillful listening is of enormous help.

I believe my ultimate gift to my family, community and the world at large, is the legacy of listening and all the transformative power it holds. I am dedicated to transforming myself and others, and leaving the world a better, richer place for me having lived and listened in it.

References

1. Tomatis, Alfred (1992). *The conscious ear*. Barrytown, NY: Station Hill Press.

2. Schwartz, C. E. and Sendor, M. (1999). Helping others helps oneself: Response shift in peer support. Social Science & Medicine, 48, No. 11, 1563-1575.

3. Lehrer, J. (2008). Deliberate practice. *The Frontal Cortex.* http://scienceblog.com/cortex/2008/07/deliberate_practice.php

4. Pearsall, Paul (2007). *The last self-help book you'll ever need*. NY: Basic Books.

5. Nichols, Ralph G. (1967). *Are you listening?* NY: McGraw-Hill.

6. Gladwell, Malcolm (2002). The naked face. *The New Yorker*, August 5th.

7. Finn, Charles C. (2002). *For the mystically inclined*. Bloomington, IN: Author House.

8. Levitin, D. (2014). *The organized mind. NY: Dutton.*

9. Scaer, Robert (2007). The dissociation capsule. http://www.committedparent.com/Dissociation.html

10. Tolle, Eckart (2004). *The power of now.* Novato, CA: New World Library.

11. Pagels, Elaine (1989). *The gnostic gospels.* NY: Vintage.

12. Hopkins, Patricia and Anderson, Sherry Ruth (1992). *The feminine face of god.* NY: Bantam.

13. Bishop, James (2004). *The day Christ was born.* NY: Harper-One.

14. Vera, Hernan and Feagin, Joe R. (Eds.)(2007). Unconscious rascism, social cognition theory, and the legal intent doctrine: The neuron fires next time. In *Handbook of the sociology of racial and ethnic relations.* NY: Springer.

15. International Listening Association home page. www.listen.org

16. Krishnamurti, J. (1989). *Think on these things*. NY: Harper Perennial.

17. Pearce, Joseph Chilton (1992). *Magical child*. NY: Plume.

18. Mate, G. (2010). *In the realm of hungry ghosts: Close encounters with addiction.* Berkeley, CA: North Atlantic Books.

19. Barr, Nevada (2004). *Seeking enlightenment hat by hat*. NY: Berkley Trade.

20. Kahneman, D. (2011). *Thinking Fast and Slow.* NY: Farrar, Strauss & Giroux.

21. Siegel, Daniel (2007). *The mindful brain.* NY: W.W. Norton.

22. Brady, Mark (2003). *The wisdom of listening.* Somerville, MA: Wisdom Publications.

Listening Skills Bibliography

Adler, Mortimer (1983). *How to Speak; How to Listen.* New York: Simon and Schuster.

Brady, Mark (Ed.) (2003). *The Wisdom of Listening.*
Somerville, MA: Wisdom Publications.

Burley-Allen, Madelyn (1995). *Listening : The Forgotten Skill (A Self-Teaching Guide).* NY: John Wiley & Son.

Ghoulston, Mark (2010). *Just listen.* NY: Amacom Publishing.

Lindahl, Kay (2003). *Practicing the Sacred Art of Listening.* Woodstock, VT: Skylight Paths Publishing.

Nichols, Michael P. (1995). *The Lost Art of Listening.* New York: The Guilford Press.

Patterson, K., Grenny, J., McMillan, R. & Switzler, A. (2002). *Crucial Conversations.* NY: McGraw-Hill.

Rosenberg, Marshall B. (2003). *Nonviolent Communication: A Language of Life.* Encinitas, CA: Puddledancer.

Shafir, Rebecca Z. (2000). *The Zen of Listening: Mindful Communication in the Age of Distraction.* Wheaton, IL: Quest Books.

Steil, Lyman and Bommelje, Rick (2004*). Listening Leaders.* Edina, MN: Beaver's Pond Press, Inc.

About the Author:

Mark Brady is an award-winning author, teacher, and trainer. He has taught graduate courses in skillful listening for the last dozen years. He has edited the listening anthology, *The Wisdom of Listening* and written numerous articles for journals and national magazines. He is the prize-winning author of a number of books. The most recent is entitled *A Father's Book of Listening*. It and the others can be ordered from bookstores or on the Internet or by emailing: paideia@gmail.com.

Contact us

We hope you enjoyed this book and the transformations taking place in your life as you've practiced some of the skills. We invite you to send us your comments, ideas and any stories you'd like to share at the addresses below. We'd be delighted to hear from you!

To contact Mark Brady for more information:
Email: doctormarkbrady@gmail.com
5489 Coles Road
Langley, WA 98260
Office: (360) 981-1410

To Order:

To order copies of *Noble Listening* send a check for $16.95 (includes shipping and handling) to: Paideia Press, 5489 Coles Road, Langley, WA 98260

(WA residents send $17.95 which includes tax and shipping.) Please remember to include your shipping information. Orders of 20 or more copies are discounted. Please contact us for pricing and shipping information.

Made in the USA
Columbia, SC
24 July 2019